SOLAR ECLIPSE 1914

Arseny Tarkovsky
Solar Eclipse 1914
SELECTED POEMS

Selected & translated by
PETER ORAM

Introduction by Boris Dralyuk &
Irina Mashinski

ARC PUBLICATIONS
2021

Published by Arc Publications,
Nanholme Mill, Shaw Wood Road,
Todmorden OL14 6DA, UK
www.arcpublications.co.uk

978 1910345 85 6 (pbk)
978 1910345 86 3 (ebk)

ACKNOWLEDGEMENTS
The publishers are grateful to Arseny Tarkovsky's granddaughter,
Marina Tarkovsky, for granting them permission to
reproduce the poems in the original Russian.
They would also like to thank Peter Oram's wife, Gudrun Oram, for her
encouragement and support throughout this project,
without which the book would never have seen the light of day.

Design by Tony Ward

'Arc Publications Classics: New Translations of Great Poets of the Past'
Series Editor: Jean Boase-Beier

CONTENTS

Translator's Preface / 9
Introduction – 'Sudden Ascent':
Arseny Trakovsky and Peter Oram / 11

Biographical Notes / 82

In preparing the translations for this selection of poetry by Arseny Tarkovsky, I have tried to identify and represent as many of the parameters of each poem as is reasonably possible, in versions which can stand up with confidence as poems in their own right while remaining true to their source. With each poem my first – and *sine qua non* – step was to make sure that every lexical unit of the poem in question was thoroughly understood. It may sound pedantic, but I'm prepared to look up the commonest of words in the fattest of dictionaries if I have the least suspicion that there is some idiosyncratic phrase associated with it that I had forgotten about or simply did not know. In the case of the present volume, I have had an additional secret weapon in the shape of Vasily Tsibulnik, a retired lecturer from Krasnodar, who has supplied a wealth of background knowledge and information.

My second preparatory step was to look at form, rhyme and metre as a kind of whole, since they represent the immediate, visible face of the poem yet at the same time are impersonal and detachable. This also in turn implies that they are not necessarily unique to the poem in hand, and thus they may be kept or cast aside at the translator's discretion. My approach, however, has been to preserve all three elements whenever I can or, if I feel unable or unwilling to accommodate them for a particular poem then, rather than just to tinker with them a bit, to make a radical change – see for example the poems 'White Day' and 'Moth'. In any case, the reader deserves at the very least to be given some clue as to how the poem appears on the page. I think it is a little unfair on the reader to lead him or her to claim that they know and love the work of Mayakovsky or Akhmatova when they have a misconceived idea of what the original even looks like. Just because quatrains, rhymed couplets and regular pentameters etc. tend to sound to contemporary ears either dated or like doggerel in English, we don't have to be embarrassed or apologetic if they turn up in poetry that we are translating. In Russian there are a number of reasons – historical, metre- and stress-related, social / demographic etc. – why such elements have continued to be common currency for many modern Russian poets, and it's of even more importance in these days of a widespread and paranoid rusophobia that western society be prepared to meet Russian culture on its own terms.

It's generally possible to divide any poem, or any text, into a number of simple and succinct statements, phrases etc., and in Tarkovsky's verse these tend to match line beginnings and endings in almost every case. A pair of lines may match main clause and dependent clause, two main clauses, statement and its simile, question and answer etc. In this situation I would tend to break up the monotonous rhythmic plod that such treatment would produce in English to ensure that phrase endings and line endings did not match, and furthermore, I would try to choose rhymes that did not fall on "important" words but on "insignificant" ones. For example, I might not rhyme "flower" with "power", but with "now a" or "how a", or even "now. A"… (Or: "Ow!!… er??"…?).

Used with discretion, extended enjambements can impart a wonderful fluidity to the text. A sprinkling of internal rhymes, and half rhymes to taste, and the translator will find the most dogged of doggerel scuttling away with its tail between its legs.

It's around this point that I tend to get stuck. I look at my watch and find that I've just spent three hours trying to find a Bengali word for a table with five legs that rhymes with 'nemesis'. And then it begins. My head goes out of control, the two halves of my brain clash together and reach critical mass, it's my nineteenth nervous breakdown. And in a deluge of richness the rhymes come tumbling in…

It would be nice if it were as easy as that. As it is, we translators of poetry just muddle along as best we can, knowing that our task is anyway an impossible one. Nevertheless, I hope that you will find pleasure in at least a few of the translations in the present selection.

Peter Oram, Schwabach, Germany, Autumn 2018

In the English-speaking world, the major Russian poet Arseny Tarkovsky is known, if he is known at all, as something of a bit player in the work of his far more famous son, the filmmaker Andrei Tarkovsky. Fans of the son's *Mirror* (1975) and *Stalker* (1979) will have heard the father's poems, piecing together their meaning from the subtitles, but are unlikely to have sought out better translations; and even if they had, they were unlikely to find translations as instantly enchanting, as subtle yet energetic as those gathered here.

It may be more surprising to learn, however, that a great many Russian readers also encountered Tarkovsky's poetic voice before they were able to read his poems. The experience of Irina Mashinski, a Russian-American poet born in Moscow in the late 1950s, helps elucidate the peculiar role Tarkovsky played in Russian literature – that of a messenger from the past who, miraculously, not only survived but remained whole, untarnished, eternally fresh.

> One time, in early spring, in one of the upper classes of secondary school, when dying of boredom during a lecture on literature, I reached over to the shelf that ran along the classroom wall and pulled down the first book my hand chanced upon – a blue-backed selection of works by the 18th-century Turkmen poet Magymguly Pyragy. I remember the warm page, brightly lit by the school-day sun, and the striking poems – not at all exotic, though "eastern", masterfully built yet at the same time alive. This sensation came and went: the pages would cool down then light up again. Taking a look at the table of contents, I discovered that all the living versions belonged to Arseny Tarkovsky. The name, which sounded beautiful in Russian, was new to me, although by that time I was already a fairly experienced reader of poetry. It is somehow natural that my first meeting with a poet destined to become one of

my favourites was not a meeting with his poems, but with his translations. The next one – this time real – happened thanks to his son's semi-prohibited films, *Mirror* and, a little later, *Stalker*, which my friends and I went to see somewhere in the Moscow suburbs. Then, unexpectedly, an LP was released – a recording of Tarkovsky reading his poems. And so it happened that Tarkovsky came to me and to many members of my generation as a voice and as an image, and only later through his books.

The charm of Tarkovsky's poems is mysterious, comparable only to the charm of his voice. Charm is not the same as popularity. Charm is like the gravity of an extremely strong, compact celestial body, a star – it is the gravity of the text and of the poetic personality behind it. A popular poet, on the other hand, is like an asteroid or planet that obediently circles around a large readership. Tarkovsky is a poet of charm, not popularity.

Tarkovsky was born on 25 June 1907 in Yelisavetgrad (now Kropyvnytskyi, Ukraine) into a family with Polish roots. His father, who had a deep interest in writing and the theatre, took both his sons to readings by some of the most illustrious poets of the Russian Silver Age – a period of cultural efflorescence that began in the 1880s and ended in the first decade of Soviet rule.

In 1921, shortly after the end of the Civil War (which claimed the life of his older brother, Valery), Tarkovsky's poetic career got off to a disastrous start. He and a group of friends published a poem in a Ukrainian newspaper that, by means of an acrostic, disparaged Lenin. They were apprehended and sent off to the regional capital, but Tarkovsky managed to escape from the train. For two years he supported himself as best he could, going from job to job – shoemaker's apprentice, fisherman – before moving to Moscow in 1925 and devoting himself to literature. For the next four years he attended a course run by the All-Russian Union of Poets, where he forged a number of lasting friendships, the most consequential of which was with the poet and literary theorist Georgy Shengeli (1894-1956).

Although Tarkovsky's poems did appear in print in the 1920s, the Stalinist cultural policies of the 1930s left little room for his brand of intimate lyricism, still rooted in the tradition of the Silver Age. Like many of his older, more established colleagues – including Anna Akhmatova, Osip Mandelstam, and Boris Pasternak – he began to write, as the Russians say, 'for the drawer'. It was Shengeli who provided him with a literary lifeline, hiring him as a translator at the State Publishing House. There, Tarkovsky and his fellow poets-turned-translators were able to hone their craft and obliquely express their own lyrical impulses by transforming literal renditions of poems from Armenia, Georgia, Central Asia, and elsewhere into Russian verse.

It was only two decades after the Second World War – where Tarkovsky was badly wounded, necessitating the amputation of a part of his leg – and a decade after Stalin's death in 1953, that a collection of his own verse, *Before the Snow* (1962), was finally permitted to appear. Its title is telling: these poems, emerging with the Thaw, seemed to have preserved the atmosphere of a warmer time through the deep freeze of the preceding quarter of a century. Irina Mashinski recalls the impact of this delayed flowering.

> Tarkovsky gained real recognition in the 1960s, when three of his books were published. But he only became truly famous – and, most importantly, beloved – in my time, in the 1970s and 1980s.
>
> A witness to his late glory, I was among those who, stomping across the trampled snow in front of the Central House of Writers, desperately tried to score tickets to his "author's evenings". I managed to see one performance, in the early '80s. Far, far away on the stage stood a tall man with a cane, reciting poems I knew by heart – which poems they were, I don't quite remember, but I'll never forget that beautiful far-away figure of an old man with a

cane, the figure of a master, whose whole aspect radiated calm dignity.

Tarkovsky's poems convey the feeling of returning to the Earth with unusual force. It's no coincidence that his second collection was titled *To Earth Its Own* (1966). On the one hand, his sense of the Earth is acutely cosmic (Tarkovsky was fond of astronomy), while on the other, it's the purely physical, tactile sense of a barefoot philosopher wandering the land. 'The book and the natural world are like two halves of one nutshell, and it's impossible to separate them without touching the meat inside,' he once wrote. His language is the language of the material world. And the charm of his poems also owes to his understanding of various crafts, his love and even deification of them. Well into old age, he could easily take apart and assemble a typewriter, mend shoes, darn and embroider socks.

For him, space and time are not the medium in which human experience takes place, they become this very experience. Even when Tarkovsky writes about the past or the future, he is writing about the present. Eternity is present in the intense experience of each moment, just as eternity was ever-present for the early Christian philosophers. The flow of time is a constant theme in Tarkovsky's poems, in which even death – of a person or of a craft – acquires the tangibility and richness of life. His verse is always in motion, never fully crystallizes, never reaches (in the Aristotelian sense) its final end – it remains alive.

The very quality that makes Tarkovsky's verse vital in Russian, its combination of earthly texture and metaphysical movement, also enlivens this book – the final gift of a marvellous poet and master translator, Peter Oram. Time and again, the English versions take off from the page, following the originals with the same sense of poetic freedom – and hence the same spiritual fidelity – that guided Tarkovsky's own translations:

A moth's sudden ascent
of a ladder of light
as if someone had switched on
his fluttering flight.

Memories of Peter, who passed away in 2019, haunted us as we read this selection – perhaps nowhere more so than in his version of 'In Memory of Friends', a poem written in 1945, forty-four years before Tarkovsky's own death on 27 May 1989. It begins:

I didn't really have that many friends,
they died, they died, and I don't really know
when their last moments came, nor do I know
which paradise I could entrust them to,
to which earth to entrust their cold remains.

At the end, Tarkovsky wonders, 'Whom can I tell which way the wind is blowing, / how green the grass is or how blue the sky?' The answer is: us, his circle of readers, which our friend Peter has generously, brilliantly broadened and extended into the future.

Boris Dralyuk and Irina Mashinski, 2021

SOLAR ECLIPSE 1914

В ЯРКИХ ПЯТНАХ СВЕТА...

В ярких пятнах света, в путанице линий путаницелиний
Я себя нашёл, как брата – брат:
Шмель пирует в самой сердцевине
Розы четырёх координат.

Я не зн аю, кто я и откуда,
Где зачат – в аду или в раю,
Знаю только, что за это чудо
Я своё бессмертье отдаю.

Ничего не помнит об отчизне,
Лепестки вселенной вороша,
Пятая координата жизни –
Самосознающая душа.

IN THE BRIGHT LIGHT-PATCHES...

In the bright light-patches and tangled lines
I discovered myself, like a twin
who sucked like a bee on the rose's heart
and the four dimensions within.

Who am I? Where do I come from?
Was I conceived in heaven or hell? –
I would rather lose my immortal soul
than the following miracle:

though we pluck off the rose-petals of our days
and our past shrinks away in the distance,
there is this: the fifth dimension: the soul
that's aware of its own existence.

Я ТАК ДАВНО РОДИЛСЯ...

Я так давно родился,
Что слышу иногда,
Как надо мной проходит
Студеная вода.

А я лежу на дне речном,
И если песню петь –
С травы начнем, песку зачерпнем
И губ не разомкнем.

Я так давно родился,
Что говорить не могу,
И го+род мне приснился
На каменном берегу.

А я лежу на дне речном
И вижу из воды
Далекий свет, высокий дом,
Зеленый луч звезды.

Я так давно родился,
Что если ты придешь
И руку положишь мне на глаза,
То это будет ложь,

А я тебя удержать не могу,
И если ты уйдешь
И я за тобой не пойду, как слепой,
То это будет ложь.

I WAS BORN SO LONG AGO...

I was born so long ago
that there are times when I
can hear somewhere above me
freezing waters rolling by.

But I lie on the river bed
and I may sing my song
with sprouting grass, with sifted sand
but do not move my tongue.

I was born so long ago
that I can speak no more
but dream about a city
upon a stony shore,

and I lie on the river bed
and, through the waters, far
above, I see a tall house, lights,
the green glow of a star.

I was born so long ago.
But should you ever try
to cover with your hands my eyes
then that would be a lie.

I lie upon the river bed:
I can't hold onto you
for if I blindly followed you
that would be lying too.

ЕСТЬ ГОРОД, НА РЕКЕ СТОИТ...

Есть город, на реке стоит,
Но рыбы нет в реке,
И нищий дремлет на мосту
С тарелочкой в руке.

Кто по мосту ходил не раз,
Тарелочку видал,
Кто дал копейку, кто пятак,
Кто ничего не дал.

А как тарелочка поёт,
Качается, звенит,
Рассказывает о себе,
о нищем говорит.

Не оловянная она,
Не тяжела руке,
Не глиняная – упадёт
Подпрыгнет налегке.

Кто по мосту ходил не раз,
Не помнит ничего,
Он город свой забыл, и мост,
И нищего того.

Но вспомнить я хочу себя,
И город над рекой.
Я вспомнить нищего хочу
С протянутой рукой, –

Когда хоть ветер
говорил с тарелочкой живой…
и город этот наяву
Остался бы со мной.

THERE IS A TOWN...

There is a town. It's on a river.
But the river has no fish.
On the bridge a beggar dozes,
in his hands a little dish.

Those who passed by now and then
would see him loitering.
Some gave a kopek, some gave five.

Some didn't give a thing.
But how this little dish can sing
and ring, and rock – it can
tell us such tales about itself
and of the beggarman!

The dish is neither tin nor clay,
nor is it heavy. When
he lets it fall by accident
it springs back up again.

Those who pass by now and then
don't recall a thing.
Forgotten: town, forgotten: bridge,
forgotten – everything.

But I want to recall that town,
recall that river, and
recall that beggar sitting there
with his outstretching hand.

I'd like to hear these winds converse
with that small dish, and then
all this could remain with me
in waking life again

.

МОТЫЛЕК

Ходит мотылек
По ступеням света,
Будто кто зажег
Мельтешенье это.

Книжечку чудес
На лугу открыли,
Порошком небес
Подсинили крылья.

В чистом пузырьке
Кровь другого мира
Светится в брюшке
Мотылька-лепира.

Я бы мысль вложил
В эту плоть, но трогать
Мы не смеем жил
Фараона с ноготь.

MOTH

A moth's sudden ascent
of a ladder of light
as if someone had switched on
his fluttering flight.

He opens his booklet
of wonders – he must
have powdered his wings
with heaven's blue dust.

In the transparent flask
of his abdomen.
flows the blood of another
world's denizen.

I could be in his body
but dare not displace
this miniature pharaoh's
resting-place.

СИНИЦЫ

В снегу, под небом синим,

                    а меж ветвей – зеленым,

Стояли мы и ждали

                    подарка на дорожке.

Синицы полетели

                    с неизъяснимым звоном,

Как в греческой кофейне

                    серебряные ложки.

Могло бы показаться

                    что там невесть откуда

Идет морская синька

                    на белый камень мола,

И вдруг из рук служанки

                    под стол летит посуда,

И ложки подбирает,

                    бранясь, хозяин с пола.

BLUETITS

White snow-beneath a pure blue sky
                    and branches tipped with green.
We walk the pathway wondering
                    what gift is waiting for us,
till crowds of fluttering bluetits
                    erupt onto the scene:
like silver Grecian coffee spoons
                    their sweetly jingling chorus.

    And suddenly – yes! a jetty
                    where we seem to stand
where blue waves fall across white rocks
                    upon some distant shore.
The waitress comes and lets the plates
                    fall from her careless hands.
The manager, disgruntled,
                    picks the spoons up from the floor.

ГОЛУБИ

Семь голубей – семь дней недели
Склевали корм и улетели,
На смену этим голубям
Другие прилетают к нам.

Живем, считаем по семерке,
В последней стае только пять,
И наши старые задворки
На небо жалко променять:

Тут н-аши сизари воркуют,
По кругу ходят и жалкуют,
Асфальт крупитчатый клюют
И на поминках дождик пьют.

PIGEONS

The seven weekdays – seven pigeons
peck at seeds, to other regions,
then return, forgotten, for
they're soon replaced by seven more.

We live and count our days in sevens,
better though to count in fives:
soon we'll exchange for some poor heaven
that backyard of our daily lives,

a heaven where our friends are doing
their endless rounds, their mournful cooing
or peck the tarmac, seeds pursuing,
where weather's wet and worse is brewing.

ГОЛУБИ НА ПЛОЩАДЬЕ

Я не хуже, не лучше других,
И на площадь хожу я со всеми
Покупать конопляное семя
И кормить голубей городских.

Потому что я вылепил их,
Потому что своими руками
Глину мял я, как мертвые в яме,
Потому что от ран штыковых

Я без просыпу спал, как другие,
В клейкой глине живых,
Потому что из глины живее России
Всем народом я вылепил их:

PIGEONS IN THE SQUARE

I'm no better – nor worse – than the others
who go to the square in the town,
 and buy hempseed for scattering down
for the pigeons which gather together.

Why? Here's the reason: I fashioned
these birds with my very own hands
like the dead gripping clay in the trenches,
while we, with our bayonet gashes,

slept on in the trenches till day,
and there, more alive than the living,
we – all of us – moulded these pigeons
out of the good Russian clay.

Девочка Серебряные Руки
Заблудилась под вечер в лесу.
В ста шагах разбойники от скуки
Свистом держат птицу на весу.

Кони спотыкаются лихие,
Как бутылки, хлопает стрельба,
Птичьи гнезда и сучки сухие
Обирает поверху судьба.

– Ой, березы, вы мои березы,
Вы мои пречистые ручьи,
Расступитесь и омойте слезы,
Расплетите косыньки мои.

Приоденьте корнем и травою,
Положите на свою кровать,
Помешайте злобе и рзабою
Руки мои белые отнять!

SILVERHANDS

Silverhands got lost one evening
in the woods in dwindling light.
Nearby, robbers, bored, with skilful
whistling stopped birds in mid-flight.

Sprightly horses stumbling, rearing…
Like popping corks the bullets fly.
Meanwhile destiny is clearing
last year's nests and twigs away.

Silver birches, step aside!
Crystal waters, wash away
these tears! I want my hair untied!
I want it hanging loose and free!

Clothe me, then, in roots and grasses!
Forget your anger! You may lay
me down upon the grassy ground
but don't take these white hands away!

У ЛЕСНИКА

В лесу потерял я ружье,
Кусты разрывая плечами;
Глаза мне ночное зверье
Слепило своими свечами.

Лесник меня прячет в избе,
Сижу я за кружкою чая,
И кажется мне, что к себе
Попал я, по лесу блуждая.

Открыла мне память моя
Таинственный мир соответствий:
И кружка, и стол, и скамья
Такие же точно, как в детстве.

Такие же двери у нас
И стены такие же были.
А он продолжает рассказ,
Свои стародавние были.

Цигарку свернет и в окно
Моими посмотрит глазами.
– Пускай их свистят. Все равно.
У нас тут балуют ночам.

IN THE WOODSMAN'S HUT

My gun is lost. Lost in the woods
I tear a passage through the tight
and tangled bushes, dazzled by
the eyes of creatures of the night.

In his hut the woodsman hides me;
for several hours I've had to roam,
but now, a mug of tea beside me
I feel as if I've just come home.

My memory reveals a world
of secret correspondences,
and mug, chair, table match exactly
those of my own childhood days.

This door's the same as my own door,
each wall resembles my own walls,
and he continues my own story
as he tells his ancient tales.

He stares out through the window through
my eyes and rolls a cigarette.
"Oh, let them whistle – I don't care!
They always fool around at night…"

ГРЕЧЕСКАЯ КОФЕЙНЯ

Где белый камень в диком блеске
Глотает синьку вод морских,
Грек Ламбринуди в красной феске
Ждал посетителей своих.

Они развешивали сети,
Распутывали поплавки
И, улыбаясь точно дети,
Натягивали пиджаки.

– Входите, дорогие гости,
Сегодня кофе, как вино! –
И долго в греческой кофейне
Гремели кости Домино.

А чашки разносила Зоя,
И что-то нежное и злое
Скрывали медленная речь,
Как будто море кружевное
Спадало с этих узких плеч.

GREEK COFFEE BAR

Where the white stone's splendid wildness
swallows the blue of the sea
waiting for guests in his crimson fez
sat old Lambrinudi.

They'd long hung up the fishing nets,
untangled lines and floats,
and smiling bright as little kids
had tightened up their coats.

"Come in, my friends, come in! Today
like wine the coffee flows!"
And in the coffee bar they played
the clattering dominoes.

But while Zoya's putting out the cups,
some tender, insidious thing
in the slow conversation quietly smoulders,
as if the waves, like a white lace shawl,
were slipping down from her narrow shoulders.

Красный фонарик стоит на снегу.
Что-то я вспомнить его не могу.

Может быть, это листок-сирота,
Может быть, это обрывок бинта,

Может быть, это на снежную шир
Вышел кружить красногрудый снегирь,

    Может быть, это морочит меня
    Дымный закат окаянного дня.

THIS RED LAMP STANDING IN THE SNOW…

This red lamp standing in the snow –
it reminds me of something. Of what? I don't know.

An autumn leaf that was left behind?
A bandage-scrap from a bleeding wound?

A red-chested bullfinch who happened to go
in circles over great fields of snow?

> – or is it a trick someone's trying to play:
> the smoke-filled end to another damned day?

ЗАСУХА

Земля зачерствела, как губы,
Обметанные сыпняком,
И засухи дымные трубы
Беззвучно гудели кругом,

И высохло русло речное,
Вода из колодцев ушла.
Навечно осталась от зноя
В крови ледяная игла.

Качается узкою лодкой,
И целится в сердце мое,
Но, видно, дороги
короткой Не может найти острие.

Есть в круге грядущего мира
Для засухи этой приют,
Где души скитаются сиро
И ложной надеждой живу

DROUGHT

The earth was arid, parched, like lips
when typhus is overcome.
The smouldering, empty waterpipes
gave out a monotonous hum.

The river was nothing but hard dry mud;
in the wells the water was gone;
like an icy needle in the blood
the terrible heat blazed on –

like a narrow boat rocking to and fro,
with my heart as its destination,
but there's no easy way to go
to reach that final station.

Where future worlds rotate there'll be
a refuge for the drought,
where orphaned souls roam aimlessly
and hope has no way out.

ЗАТМЕНИЕ СОЛНЦА 1914

В то лето народное горе
Надело железную цепь,
И тлела по самое море
Сухая и пыльная степь,

И под вечер горькие дали,
Как душная бабья душа,
Багровой тревогой дышали
И бога хулили, греша.

А утром в село на задворк
Пришел дезертир босиком,
В белесой своей гимнастерке,
С голодным и темным лицом,

И, словно из церкви икона,
Смотрел он, как шел на ущерь
По ржавому дну небосклона
Алмазный сверкающий серп.

Запомнил я взгляд без движенья,
Совсем из державы иной,
И понял печать отчужденья
В глазах, обожженных войной.

И стало темно. И в молчанье,
Зеленом, глубоком как сон,
Ушел он и мне на прощанье
Оставил ружейный патрон.

Но сразу, по первой примете,
Узнал ослепительный свет…

… ного я прожил на свете! Столетие! Тысячу лет!

SOLAR ECLIPSE 1914

In that summer a nation in mourning
was bound in iron chains,
and smouldering all the way down to the sea
lay the dry and dusty plains.

And like a stifled woman's soul
the land, as evening came,
breathed its blood-red warning out
and cursed god's holy name.

At the edge of a little village
a deserter came into sight,
barefoot, and with a cold, dark face,
his tunic faded white.

And, as if through the eyes of an icon,
he watched as the diamond light
of the brilliant sickle low in the skies
narrowed then vanished from sight.

And recalling that motionless moment
from a world unlike any before,
I understood that alien stamp
in eyes that are scorched by war.

And darkness fell. He departed.
And as a kind of farewell
in the silence, deep and green as sleep,
he left me a rifle shell.

And suddenly – that brilliant light…
I'd fathomed it to the core…

How long I've lived! A hundred years!…
              … A thousand years or more!

БЕЖЕНЕЦ

Не пожалела на дорогу соли,
Так насолила, что свела с ума.
Горишь, святая камская зима,
А я живу один, как ветер в поле.

Скупишься, мать, дала бы хлеба, что ли,
Полны ядреным снегом закрома,
Бери да ешь. Тяжка моя сума;
Полпуда горя и ломоть недоли.

Я ноги отморожу на ветру,
Я беженец, я никому не нужен,
Тебе-то все равно, а я умру.

Что делать мне среди твоих жемчужин
И кованного стужей серебра
На черной Каме, ночью, без костра?

REFUGEE

You gave me salt to take upon my way.
Oh, too much salt! I almost went insane!
I live alone, like wind across the plain.
Burn, Kama-River winter! Burn away!

You could at least have been so free with bread!
But now your granaries are filled with snow.
My bag's half-full of ice, half-full of woe.
Take! And eat! – It weighs me down like lead.

The icy wind bites at my feet. Yes, I
am just a refugee, no use at all
to anyone! You don't care if I die!

Among your pearls of snow, your icicles
of beaten silver where is there respite
beside the Kama, fireless, at night?

ДОЖДЬ

Как я хочу вдохнуть в стихотворенье
Весь этот мир, меняющий обличье:
Травы неуловимое движенье,

Мгновенное и смутное величье
ревьев, раздраженный и крылатый
Сухой песок, щебечущий по-птичьи –

Весь этот мир, прекрасный и горбатый,
Как дерево на берегу Ингула.
Там я услышал первые раскаты

Грозы. Она в бараний рог согнула
Упрямый ствол, и я увидел крону
Зеленый слепок грозового гула.

А дождь бежал по глиняному склону,
Гонимый стрелами, ветвисторогий,
Уже во всем подобный Актеону.

У ног моих он пал на полдороге.

RAIN

How I would like to breathe into my verses
this whole world with its constant restlessness,
the tiny movements of the meadow grasses,

the grandeur, vague but instantaneous,
of trees, or birds that rise into the sky,
like swirls of sand in twittering nervousness –

this whole world that's so splendidly awry,
like that tree beside the Ingul River
where I first heard the thunder crack the sky.

It bent the trunk into the twisting of
a ram's horn; looking up into the crown
I saw the thunder's image copied over

and on the clayey slopes the rain poured down
with ragged lightning darts in hot pursuit
as Actaeon was once pursued by hounds.

I saw him fall before me at my feet.

Их так немного было у меня,
Все умерли, все умерли. Не знаю,
Какому раю мог бы я доверить
Последнее дыханье их. Не знаю,
Какой земле доверить мог бы я
Этот холодный прах. Одним огнем
Нам опалило щеки. Мы делили
Одну судьбу. Они достойней были
И умерли, а я еще живу.
Но я не стану их благодарить
За дивный дар, мне выпавший на долю
Я не хотел столь дорогой ценой
Купить его. Мне – их благодарить?
Да разве я посмею им признаться,
Что я дышу, и вдовы их глядят
В глаза мои – пусть не в глаза, а мимо –
Признаться им – без укоризны? Нет,
Я вдов не очерню пред мертвецами
Вдова пройдет сторонкою и скажет…
Им всё равно, что скажут вдовы их.
Благодарить за то, что я хотел бы
На их могилы принести цветы
В живых руках, дыша благоуханьем,
За шагом шаг ступая по траве,
По их траве, когда они лежат
В сырой земле и двинуться не могут.
Что двинуться? Когда их больше нет.
Ни я, ни вы, никто не нужен им.
А я без них – с кем буду хлеб делить,
С кем буду пить вино в мой светлый день,
Кому скажу: какой сегодня ветер,
Как зелена трава и небо сине?

IN MEMORY OF FRIENDS

I didn't really have that many friends
they died, they died, and I don't really know
when their last moments came, nor do I know
which paradise I could entrust them to,
to which earth to entrust their cold remains.
One fire burned all our cheeks, we shared a single
destiny, but they were worthier
and died. I am, however, still alive –
a wondrous gift, but one for which I cannot
ever thank them – a gift from heaven, for which
I wish I'd never paid so high a price.
Thank them?... I don't even dare to tell them
that I'm still breathing. Whether their widows look me
in the eye, or whether they avoid
my gaze, how can I possibly admit it
without feeling their reproach – and for my friends' sake
I cannot insult them.
Sometimes a widow may pass by and say...
... but what difference does it make to them,
whatever they say? Or should I thank them for my being
able to bring flowers to their graves
with living hands, spreading fragrance, passing
step by step across the grass, their grass,
while they lie underneath it in the damp earth,
incapable of movement?
What movement – when there's nothing left to move?
They have no further use for you or me.
And I have no one left to share my bread with,
no one to drink wine with in the dazzling day.
Whom can I tell which way the wind is blowing,
how green the grass is or how blue the sky?

СТОЛ НАКРЫТ НА ШЕСТЕРЫХ...

Стол накрыт на шестерых
Розы да хрусталь...
А среди гостей моих
Горе да печаль.

И со мною мой отец,
И со мною брат.
Час проходит. Наконец
У дверей стучат.

Как двенадцать лет назад,
Холодна рука
И немодные шумят
Синие шелка.

И вино поет из тьмы,
И звенит стекло:
"Как тебя любили мы,
Сколько лет прошло".

Улыбнется мне отец
Брат нальет вина,
Даст мне руку без кол
Скажет мне она:

"Каблучки мои в пыли,
Выцвела коса,
И поют из-под земли
Наши голоса."

ROSES IN CRYSTAL...

Roses in crystal.
The table's set – though
of the six guests expected
one's sorrow, one's woe.

My brother sits near me,
my father too. More
than an hour disappears:
there's a knock at the door.

I recall your hand's coldness.
Twelve years gone, I guess.
You were wearing your old-fashioned
rustling blue dress.

There's a clinking of glasses.
A voice starts to sing:
How years pass! How we loved you
above everything…

My brother will smile:
while father sips wine
she will hold out a hand
that bears no ring of mine,

and she'll say: 'this I'm saying
from under earth's crust:
My hair's slowly greying.
My dance-shoes are dust.'

ВОТ И ЛЕТО ПРОШЛО...

Вот и лето прошло,
Словно и не бывало.
На пригреве тепло.
Только этого мало.

Все, что сбыться могло,
Мне, как лист пятипалый,
Прямо в руки легло,
Только этого мало.

Пнапрасну ни зло,
Ни добро не пропало,
Все горело светло,
Только этого мало.

Жизнь брала под крыло,
Берегла и спасала,
Мне и вправду везло.
Только этого мало.

Листьев не обожгло,
Веток не обломало...
День промыт, как стекло,
Только этого мало.

SO THE SUMMER HAS RUN...

So the summer has run
past its sell-by date.
We were warmed by its sun
but too little too late.

All that happened – like leaves,
cinquefoliate –
lay snug in our palms but
too little too late.

There were bad times and tough
at the usual rate;
things burned brightly enough
but too little too late.

Safely under its wings
life carried our weight,
transported us safely –
too little too late.

Twigs wouldn't snap
nor leaves conflagrate.
Days glistened like glass.
But too little too late.

Я боюсь, что слишком поздно
Стало сниться счастье мне.
Я боюсь, что слишком поздно
Потянулся я к беззвездной
И чужой твоей стране.

Мне-то ведомо, какою –
Ночью темной, без огня,
Мне-то ведомо, какою
Неспокойной, молодою
Ты бываешь без меня.

Я-то знаю, как другие,
В поздний час моей тоски,
Я-то знаю, как другие
Смотрят в эти роковые,
Слишком темные зрачк

И в моей ночи ревнивой
Каблучки твои стучат,
И в моей ночи ревнивой
Над тобою дышит диво
Первых оттепелей чад.

Был и я когда-то молод.
Ты пришла из тех ночей.
Был и я когда-то молод,
Мне понятен душный холод,
Вешний лед в крови твоей.

I'M AFRAID IT'S TOO LATE NOW...

I'm afraid it's too late now
to look in dreams for happiness.
I'm afraid it's too late now
to try reach my arms out to
your land of alien starlessness.

Don't think that it's not clear to me
how in the dark and fireless night
don't think that it's not clear to me
how young, how restless you would be
if I were safely out of sight.

I'm well aware how other men
in my so late and anguished hours
I'm well aware how other men
will lose themselves entirely in
those fatal, too-dark eyes of yours.

In jealous nights I hear your heels,
your little heels re-echoing,
the tapping of your pretty heels,
while over you the world exhales,
rejoicing in the thaws of spring.

But I was also young once, and
at night you used to come to me.
Yes, I was young, and understand
your frozen blood, I understand
this iciness that stifles me.

СНЫ

Садится ночь на подоконник,
Очки волшебные надев,
И длинный вавилонский сонник,
Как жрец, читает нараспев.

ходят вверх ее ступени,
Но нет перил над пустотой,
Где судят тени, как на сцене,
Иноязычный разум твой.

Ни смысла, ни числа, ни меры.
А судьи кто? И в чем твой грех?
Мы вышли из одной пещеры
И клинопись одна на всех.

Явь от потопа до Эвклида
Мы досмотреть обречены.
Отдай – что взял; что видел – выдай!
Тебя зовут твои сыны.

И ты на чьем-нибудь пороге
Найдешь когда-нибудь приют,
Пока быки бредут, как боги,
Боками трутся на дороге
И жвачку времени жуют.

DREAMS

Night settles down at the window,
puts its magic spectacles on,
and reads like a priest at some old pagan feast
from the dreambook of Babylon.

A stairway leads ever on upwards
with no banister over the void
where as if in a play shadows judge your beha-
viour in tongues hitherto unemployed.

You can't fathom, it count it, explain it
who is judging, and what is your crime?
We're all cavemen – terrific! – and thus hieroglyphics
are ours till the end of time!

It is clear, from the flood or from Euclid:
we're ever condemned to spectate.
What life brought you – return, what it taught you – unlearn,
for the next generations await.

Some day on some road you're pursuing
you'll find some kind of sanctuary –
while bulls, godlike, mooing
plod on jostling, chewing
the cud of eternity.

Снова я на чужом языке
Пересуды какие-то слышу,
То ли это плоты на реке,
То ли падают листья на крышу

Осень, видно, и впрямь хороша.
То ли это она колобродит,
То ли злая живая душа
Разговоры с собою заводит,

То ли сам я к себе не првык…
Плыть бы мне до чужих понизовий,
Петь бы мне, как поет плотовщик,
Побольней, потемней, победовей,

На плоту натянуть дождевик
Петь бы, шапку надвинув на брови,
–Как поет на реке плотовщик
О своей невозвратной любови.

I hear the sound of gossip in
a tongue I have no knowledge of,
of rafts that splash along a stream,
or leaves that fall upon a roof.

Autumn seems the perfect time
for mischief-making, causing trouble:
living creatures lose their temper,
argue with their inner double.

Perhaps I haven't quite adjusted –
ought to sail the river's length
and sing the song the raftsman sings
but with more darkness, pain and strength

I'm on a raft, pull on my raincoat,
pull my cap down on my brow,
and sing, just like the raftsman sings,
of love and love's unanswered vows.

НОЧНАЯ РАБОТА

Свет зажгу, на чернильные пятна
Погляжу и присяду к столу,
Пусть поёт, как сверчок непонятно,
Электрический счётчик в углу.

Пусть голодные мыши скребутся,
Словно шастать им некогда днём,
И часы надо мною смеются
На дотошном наречье своём, –

Я возьмусь за работу ночную,
И пускай их до белого дня
Обнимаются напропалую,
Пьют вино, кто моложе меня.

Что мне в том? Непочатая глыба,
На два века труда предо мной.
Может, кто-нибудь скажет спасибо
За постылый мой подвиг ночной.ой.

NIGHT WORK

I'll turn the light on, sit down at my table,
stare at the inkstains, idly listening
to the electric meter's cricket-like
and incoherent song – well, let it sing

and let the hungry mice continue scratching
as if they'd had no time to scratch all day
and who cares if the clock keeps laughing at me
in its meticulous and boring way.

And so I shall begin my nightly duties
and let all those who are less old than I
fall recklessly into each others arms
and drink their wine until bright day comes by.

Who cares? I have a pile of work to do –
enough to fill a couple of centuries.
Will anyone, I wonder, ever thank me
for all the hateful and heroic nights like these?

ПАУЛЬ КЛЕЕ

Жил да был художник Пауль Клее
Где-то за горами, над лугами.
Он сидел себе один в************
С разноцветными карандашами,

Рисовал квадраты и крючочки,
Африку, ребенка на перроне,
Дьяволенка в голубой сорочке,
Звезды и зверей на небосклоне.

Не хотел он, чтоб его рисунки
Были честным паспортом природы,
Где послушно строятся по струнке
Люди, кони, города и воды,

Он хотел, чтоб линии и пятна,
Как кузнечики в июльском звоне,
Говорили слитно и понятно.
И однажды утром на картоне

Проступили крылышки и темя:
Ангел смерти стал обозначаться.
Понял Клее, что настало время
С музой и знакомыми прощаться.

Попрощался и скончался Клее.
Ничего не может быть печальней!
Если б Клее был намного злее,
Ангел смерти был бы натуральней,

PAUL KLEE

Somewhere beyond the hills, on the plateau,
there lived a certain Paul Klee, painter, who
would gather up his coloured pencils, go
and sit alone upon some avenue,

and he would draw his little hooks and squares
or children waiting for a train, or views
of Africa, or wild beasts, or stars
on the horizon, or demons dressed in blue.

He didn't want his drawings, though, to be
a slavish copy of the world around,
a plain, straightforward, personal ID
for people, ponies, waterways and towns:

he wanted all those lines and marks to ring
like crickets chirping on a summer's day,
to be intelligible and clear, to sing
as one. But one day on the page there lay

a crown, and wings: Klee knew that this was some
inscription from Death's Angel: He could tell
his time was over and the day had come
to bid his muse and all his friends farewell.

And so he took his leave and breathed his last,
and that's perhaps the saddest thing of all:
for if he'd been a man of meaner cast
Death's Angel's visit might seem natural

И тогда с художником все вместе
ы бы тоже сгинули со света,
äПорастряс бы ангел наши кости!
Но скажите мне: на что нам это?

На погосте хуже, чем в музее,
Где порой вы бродите, живые,
И висят рядком картины Клее
Голубые, желтые, блажные...

… but then, together with the painter, we
would also have to vanish from the scene.
Death's Angel would be swamped with bones. Well, we
might wonder what all this is meant to mean…

a graveyard? No – to stroll through a museum
while still alive is clearly more auspicious,
where Paul Klee's paintings hang and you can see 'em
in all their glory – yellows! Blues!… capricious!

БАЛЕТ

Пиликает скрипка, гудит барабан,
И флейта свистит по-эльзасски,
На сцену въезжает картонный рыдван
С раскрашенной куклой из сказки.

Оттуда ее вынимает партнер,
Под ляжку подставив ей руку,
И тащит силком на гостиничный двор
К пиратам на верную муку.

Те точат кинжалы, и крутят усы,
И топают в такт каблуками,
Карманные враз вынимают часы
И дико сверкают белками, –

Мол, резать пора! Но в клубничном трико,
В своем лебедином крахмале,
Над рампою прима взлетает легк
И что-то вибрирует в зале.

Сценической чуши магический ток
Находит, как свист соловьиный,
И пробует волю твою на зубок
Холодный расчет балерины.

И весь этот пот, этот грим, этот клей,
Смущавшие вкус твой и чувства,
Уже завладели душою твоей.
Так что же такое искусство?

Наверно, будет угадана связь
Меж сценой и Дантовым адом,
Иначе откуда бы площадь взялась
Со всей этой шушерой рядом?

BALLET

The scraping of fiddles, the rumble of drums,
the piccolo whistles a tune
and the facepainted fairy-tale heroine comes
in a coach made of cardboard, and soon

her partner appears, plucks her out of it, then
seizing hold of her under the thigh,
he manhandles her off to the yard of an inn
where the pitiless pirates stand by.

They sharpen their cutlasses, twirl their moustaches,
tap heels to the music's reprise
then all of a sudden they take out their watches,
a glint in the whites of their eyes

It's time for the kill! But in starchy-white swan suit
and strawberry-coloured tricot
the principal dancer flies lightly off over
the footlights; the crowd murmurs: ohhh!

The whole of this silly theatrical thrill
like a nightingale tricks your emotions.
and your will starts to fold at the lead dancer's cold
and perfected mechanical motions.

The smell of the sweat and the greasepaint and glue
may trouble your sensitive heart,
and though it may threaten to captivate you,
you wonder: can all this be art?

Between all of this and old Dante's Inferno
may parallels surely be found:
in here, as out there, is it not the town square
with all of the riffraff around?

МЕРКНЕТ ЗРЕНИЕ – СИЛА МОЯ...

Меркнет зрение – сила моя,
Два незримых алмазных копья;
Глохнет слух, полный давнего грома
И дыхания отчего дома;

Жестких мышц ослабели узлы,
Как на пашне седые волы;
И не светятся больше ночами
Два крыла у меня за плечами.

Я свеча, я сгорел на пиру.
Соберите мой воск поутру,
И подскажет вам эта страница,
Как вам плакать и чем вам гордиться

Как веселья последнюю треть
Раздарить и легко умереть,
И под сенью случайного крова
Загореться посмертно, как слово.

MY EYES GROW DIM...

My eyes grow dim – once strong and clear,
each was a secret diamond spear.
My ears, once thunder-filled, grow weak:
as child I heard the silence speak

These muscles too are useless now –
an aging ox too frail to plough,
and from my shoulders no more shine,
when night grows dark, those wings of mine.

I was a candle at your feast:
at dawn you'll clear my waxen waste.
This page may give you some ideas
on feeling pride or weeping tears.

May I die easy when I die
and, far from home, may I, when I
have shared life's happy final third,
blaze forth as the immortal word!

СОКРАТ

Я не хочу ни власти над людьми,
Ни почестей, ни войн победоносных.
Пусть я застыну, как смола на соснах,
Но я не царь, я из другой семьи.

Дано и вам, мою цикуту пьющим,
Пригубить немоту и глухоту.
Мне рубище раба не по хребту,
Я не один, но мы еще в грядущем.

Я плоть от вашей плоти, высота
Всех гор земных и глубина морская.
Как раковину мир переполняя,
Шумит по-олимпийски пустота

SOCRATES

Though I grow stiff as resin in the pine,
I have no wish for power over others
nor victories nor fame – I'm not another
tsar: I come from quite a different line.

They're destined for you too, these hemlock flowers,
you too will sip, know what it is to be
deaf-mute. I won't wear rags of slavery,
I'm one of many, and the future's ours.

For I'm flesh of your flesh – and higher than
all the mountains, deeper than any ocean.
The world's a shell filled with an emptiness
that rings, that roars – alive, Olympian:

ОКНА

Еще мои руки не связаны,
Глаза не взглянули в последний,
Последние рифмы не сказаны,
Не пахнет венками в передней

Наверчены звездные линии
На северном полюсе мира,
И прямоугольная, синяя
В окно мое вдвинута лира.

А ниже – бульвары и здания
В кристальном скрипичном напеве,
Как будущее, как сказание,
Как Будда у матери в чреве.

FROM A WINDOW

Still my hands remain unchained,
my final glance has yet to fall,
my final rhymes are still unpenned,
no scent of wreaths hangs in the hall.

Around the silver pole rotate
the stars in their bright retinue:
I watch the Lyre navigate
into my window's square of blue.

Buildings, streets are sleeping in
a violin's crystal song below,
like the future, like a legend
like the Buddha in utero.

Просыпается тело,
Напрягается слух.
Ночь дошла до предела,
Крикнул третий петух.

Сел старик на кровати,
Заскрипела кровать.
Было так при Пилате,
Что теперь вспоминать?

И какая досада
Сердце точит с утра?
И на что это надо
Горевать за Петра?

Кто всего мне дороже,
Всех желаннее мне?
В эту ночь – от кого же
Я отрекся во сне?

Крик идет петушиный
В первой утренней мгле
Через горы-долины
По широкой земле.

THE BODY SLOWLY WAKENS...

The body slowly wakens,
the sense of hearing grows,
the bounds of night are broken,
three times the cockerel crows.

The old man sits up in his bed.
The bed springs squeak and squeal
just as they did in Pilate's time...
– (that's really no big deal.)

It vexes him to feel again
his heart's unsteady beat
– a little puzzling too this grief
he's feeling for St Pete.

Who was it meant the most to me,
held me in most esteem?
And who was it that I denied
last night in that strange dream?

The cockerel won't stop crowing,
   he crows for all he's worth
      in morning's gloom through hill and dale
         – throughout this whole wide earth.

Я ТЕНЬ ИЗ ТЕХ ТЕНЕЙ, КОТОРЫЕ, ОДНАЖДЫ...

Я тень из тех теней, которые, однажды
Испив земной воды, не утолили жажды
И возвращаются на свой тернистый путь,
Смущая сны живых, живой воды глотнуть.

Как первая ладья из чрева океана,
Как жертвенный кувшин выходит из кургана,
Так я по лестнице взойду на ту сту+пень,
Где будет ждать меня твоя живая тень.

– А если это ложь, а если это сказка,
И если не лицо, а гипсовая маска
Глядит из-под земли на каждого из нас
Камнями жесткими своих бесслезных глаз…

I'M A SHADOW, ONE OF MANY, WHO...

I'm a shadow, one of many, who
drank from earth's springs and was not sated, then
returned therefore to that hard, stony path
to haunt men's dreams, drink from life's springs again.

Like ritual urns unearthed from burial-chambers,
like ships born from the womb of open sea,
I'll find myself appearing on that stairway,
and climb to where your shadow waits for me.

And if it's all a lie, a fairy tale,
if in the end your face turns out to be
a plaster mask, will you stare out at us
from eyes of stone that neither move nor see?

СЛОВО

Слово только оболочка,
Плёнка, звук пустой, но в нём
Бьётся розовая точка,
Странным светится огнём,

Бьётся жилка, вьётся живчик,
А тебе и дела нет,
Что в сорочке твой счастливчик
Появляется на свет.

Власть от века есть у слова,
И уж если ты поэт,
И когда пути другого
У тебя на свете нет,

Не описывай заране
Ни сражений, ни любви,
Опасайся предсказаний,
Смерти лучше не зови!

Слово только оболочка,
Плёнка жребиев людских,
На тебя любая строчка
Точит нож в стихах твоих.

WORDS

A word is just a shell, a skin,
an empty sound, no more,
and yet a strange flame burns within
its pink, pulsating core,

intense, alive, a throbbing vein,
yet you don't realise
the wonder of each word you write
revealed before your eyes.

Each holds the power of centuries:
if you're a poet, if you
are sure, quite sure you have no choice,
no other path will do,

don't write of things unknown, of love
or battles in advance,
avoid predictions, and don't summon
death – don't take a chance,

for though each word is just a shell,
is just a skin, it stores
your destiny – waits, hones its blades
in every line of yours.

СТИХИ ПОПАДАЮТ...

Стихи попадают в печать,
И в точках, расставленных с толком,
Себя невозможно признать
Бессонниц моих кривотолкам.

И это не книга моя,
А в дальней дороге без весел
Идет по стремнине ладья,
Что сам я у пристани бросил.

И нет ей опоры верней,
Чем дружбы неведомой плечи.
Минувшее ваше, как свечи,
До встречи погашено в ней.

EACH COMMA PLACED EXACTLY RIGHT...

Each comma placed exactly right,
my poems appear on bookshop shelves:
those murmurings of sleepless night
can barely recognize themselves!

This cannot be the book I wrote!,
the one I pushed out from the shore
to brave the swirling stream, to float
without a rudder or an oar...

> it could not find more true support
> than your strong shoulders, unknown friends.
> It bears your past, like guttering flames
> until the day we meet again.

ARSENY ALEKSANDROVICH TARKOVSKY (1907-1989) is one of the more striking Soviet authors to emerge from the post-Stalinist "thaw" period of the early 1960s. His philosophical verse was influenced by the Russian Acmeists Anna Akhmatova and Marina Tsvetayeva, filtered through his own modern sensibilty.

Tarkovsky was born in Yelisavetgrad, Russia. A brilliant linguist, specializing in Asian and Middle Eastern languages, he published his first literary translations in 1932 and worked in this field most of his life; his renderings of the Armenian bard Sayat Nova are still popular in his country.

During World War II he rose to the rank of captain in the Red Army and lost a leg in battle. The publication of Tarkovsky's first book of original poetry was halted in 1946 after the Central Committee's sweeping attack of current Soviet Literature; it would not see print until 1962, under the title *Before the Snow*. Akhmatova called it "a precious gift to the contemporary reader". His other collections are *To Earth Its Own* (1966), *Messenger* (1969), *Verses* (1974), *Winter Day* (1980), *Selected Works* (1982), *Verses of Different Years* (1983), *From Youth to Senility* (1987), and *The Blessed Light* (1993, after his death).

Tarkovsky was posthumously awarded the USSR State Prize in 1989 and now lies in a grave of honor next to author Boris Pasternak. He can be heard reciting his poetry in the films *Mirror* (1975) and *Stalker* (1979), both directed by his son, Andrei Tarkovsky.

Peter Oram (1947-2019) was born in Cardiff in 1947. He held first class honour degrees in Modern Languages (Cardiff) and Music (Aberystwyth) and an M.Mus in composition.

His publications include the novels *Maddocks* (Gomer Press, 1998), and *The Rub* (Starborn Books, 2001), a collection of poems by Russian poets on Russian poets, *The Page and the Fire,* translated from the Russian (Arc, 2007), three volumes of Rilke's French poetry in English translation, and two volumes of poetry, *White* and *Tease it Free* (Starborn, 2001 and 2012). His poems and short stories appeared in numerous magazines and anthologies.

Peter Oram lived in London, in Spain and, for many years, in Pembrokeshire, but from 2001, lived in Southern Germany. He died in 2019.

Boris Dralyuk is the editor-in-chief of the *Los Angeles Review of Books.* He is co-editor (with Robert Chandler and Irina Mashinski) of *The Penguin Book of Russian Poetry,* editor of *1917: Stories and Poems from the Russian Revolution* and *Ten Poems from Russia,* and translator of Isaac Babel, Andrey Kurkov, Maxim Osipov, Leo Tolstoy, Mikhail Zoshchenko, and other authors. His poems have appeared or are forthcoming in *The New York Review of Books, The New Criterion, The Yale Review, The Hopkins Review,* and elsewhere.

Irina Mashinski is the author of ten books of poetry in Russian. She is co-editor (with Robert Chandler and Boris Dralyuk) of *The Penguin Book of Russian Poetry* and of *Cardinal Points,* a journal of Slavic literature in translation. Her poems and essays have been translated into several languages and have appeared in *Poetry International, Plume, World Literature Today, Asymptote,* and elsewhere. Her first two books in English, *The Naked World* and *Giornata,* are forthcoming in 2021.